# CREATIVE & CRAFTING
# PRINT IT!
## Super Simple Crafts for Kids

Super Sandcastle
An Imprint of Abdo Publishing
abdobooks.com

Tamara JM Peterson
Ruthie Van Oosbree

# abdobooks.com

Published by Abdo Publishing, a division of ABDO, PO Box 398166, Minneapolis, Minnesota 55439. Copyright © 2023 by Abdo Consulting Group, Inc. International copyrights reserved in all countries. No part of this book may be reproduced in any form without written permission from the publisher. Super SandCastle™ is a trademark and logo of Abdo Publishing.

Printed in the United States of America, North Mankato, Minnesota
102022
012023

THIS BOOK CONTAINS RECYCLED MATERIALS

Design: Tamara JM Peterson, Mighty Media, Inc.
Production: Mighty Media, Inc.
Editor: Rebecca Amundson
Cover Photographs: Mighty Media, Inc.
Interior Photographs: Ferdinand Feys/Flickr, p. 7 (mural); iStockphoto, pp. 4 (both), 5 (both), 8 (all), 9 (all), 10 (girl); Mighty Media, Inc., pp. 1, 10, 11, 14, 15, 16, 17, 18, 19, 20, 21, 22, 23, 24, 25, 26, 27, 28, 29, 30, 31; Shutterstock Images, pp. 6 (boy, man), 7 (screen printing), 12 (both), 13 (both), 30 (boy); Wikimedia Commons, p. 7 (Bagh printing)
Design Elements: Mighty Media, Inc.; Shutterstock Images

Library of Congress Control Number: 2022940656

**Publisher's Cataloging-in-Publication Data**

Names: Peterson, Tamara JM; Van Oosbree, Ruthie, authors.
Title: Print it! super simple crafts for kids / by Tamara JM Peterson and Ruthie Van Oosbree
Description: Minneapolis, Minnesota : Abdo Publishing, 2023 | Series: Creative crafting | Includes online resources and index.
Identifiers: ISBN 9781532199882 (lib. bdg.) | ISBN 9781098275082 (ebook)
Subjects: LCSH: Printmaking--Juvenile literature. | Crafts (Handicrafts)--Juvenile literature. | Prints--Technique--Juvenile literature.
Classification: DDC 769--dc23

Super SandCastle™ books are created by a team of professional educators, reading specialists, and content developers around five essential components— phonemic awareness, phonics, vocabulary, text comprehension, and fluency—to assist young readers as they develop reading skills and strategies and increase their general knowledge. All books are written, reviewed, and leveled for guided reading and early reading intervention programs for use in shared, guided, and independent reading and writing activities to support a balanced approach to literacy instruction.

# CONTENTS

Printing . . . . . . . . . . . . . . . . . . . 4
Get Inspired . . . . . . . . . . . . . . . . 6
Materials . . . . . . . . . . . . . . . . . . 8
Tips & Techniques . . . . . . . . . . . 10
Becoming a Crafter . . . . . . . . . . 12
    Peaceful Printed Pillowcase . . . 14
    Photosensitive Nature Prints . . 16
    Hand-Carved Stamp Art . . . . . 18
    Ebru T-Shirt . . . . . . . . . . . . . . 20
    Hot Glue Stamps . . . . . . . . . . 22
    Stamp Bandanna . . . . . . . . . . 24
    Screen Printing Stencil . . . . . . 26
    Screen-Printed T-Shirt . . . . . . 28
Keep Crafting . . . . . . . . . . . . . . 30
Glossary . . . . . . . . . . . . . . . . . . 32

# PRINTING

Printing involves creating a **design** or image on a surface like paper or **fabric**. PRINTING INCLUDES MANY ART FORMS!

## MANY METHODS

Creating printed art is sometimes called printmaking. Stamping is one form of printmaking. Screen printing is another. Printed art also includes inking, **etching**, and photography. Artists print on paper, wood, fabric, and more. They use many tools. Some print artists use computers. They make works called graphic art.

## PRINT HISTORY

**Engraving** is an early form of printing. About 5,000 years ago, people engraved **designs** on **cylinder** stones. Then they rolled the stones over soft clay. This **transferred** the designs onto the clay.

The first paper was made about 2,000 years ago. People started printing on paper. In the 1040s, Chinese artist Bi Sheng made prints in a new way. He used blocks carved with letters and symbols. This allowed many copies of one design to be printed. Block printing advanced in later years.

## MODERN PRINTS

Today's print artists use many tools. These include digital photography, rubber stamps, special inks, and more. Print artists make all kinds of art. Modern prints are found everywhere from tote bags and book covers to billboards and art museums!

# GET INSPIRED

Artists worldwide make all kinds of printed art. Their work may INSPIRE YOUR OWN CREATIONS!

In 2022, the city of San José, California, displayed the 100 Block **Mural** Project. It included the work of 100 artists!

Some artists print on glass. This involves using both a tool and a special chemical to **etch** into the glass.

Screen printing first began in China. The process involves pushing paint into a **stencil**. This creates a **design** on the flat material underneath.

Bagh printing is a **traditional** way of printing in India. Bagh printers use wooden blocks to hand-print designs on **fabric**.

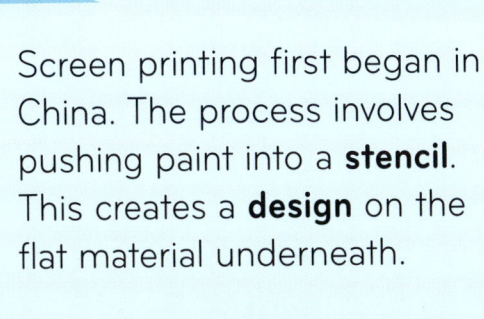

American artist Caledonia Curry is known as Swoon. She creates art on a large scale. This includes huge **linoleum** blocks and paper cutouts. Swoon applies these to walls and buildings as street art.

# MATERIALS

Gather these common tools and supplies for **PRINTING PROJECTS.**

T-shirts

foam brush

brayer

fabric ink

frame with screen

stencils

# TIPS & TECHNIQUES

Sometimes a small change can make a **BIG DIFFERENCE.**

Be safe with rubber carving tools! Carve away from yourself. Keep your hands out of the way.

Some printing **techniques** print backward onto a surface. Use a mirrored **design** in these cases. This way, the final product shows up the way you want it to!

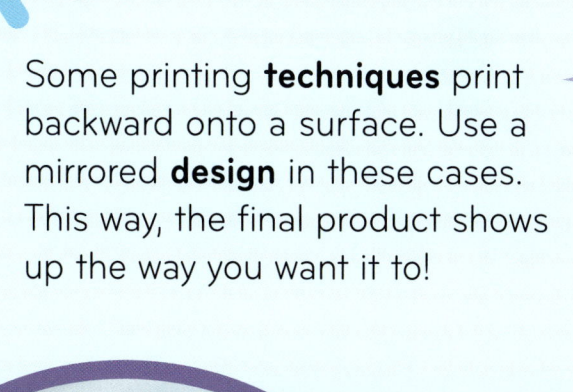

Let each part of a print dry before beginning work on the next part. This prevents wet ink or paint from smearing.

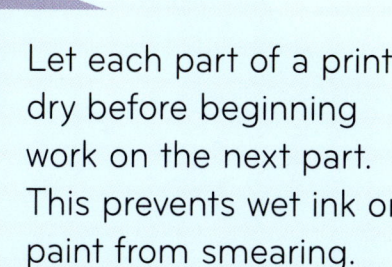

# BECOMING A CRAFTER

Become a skilled crafter with these tips. They will help your creations **TURN OUT GREAT!**

## Choose a Creative Space

A great workspace has:

- a clean, hard, flat surface
- good lighting
- comfortable seating
- an adult's OK to use!

## Get Prepped

Prepare before beginning a project!

- Read materials and tools lists.
- Gather or stock up on needed items.
- Store and organize items in containers.

## Brainstorm & Troubleshoot

Are you out of materials? Is something not turning out?

- Look at materials you have. Can any be swapped in for a missing item?
- If a step isn't working, stop and think. Can you undo the step? Can you try again?
- Ask a friend, family member, or classmate for help or ideas.

## Craft Safely

Keep safe when creating!

- Ask for help with sharp or hot tools.
- Use tools and materials the way they are meant to be used.
- Wear hand and eye protection as needed.

## Clean Up

How you close down your workspace is important.

- Put away tools and materials.
- Clean up spills and scraps.
- Store your work in a safe spot.

# PEACEFUL PRINTED PILLOWCASE

Create **stencils** to print a pillowcase that dreams are made of!

### MATERIALS
- paper
- pencil
- washed blank pillowcase
- large piece of cardboard
- poster board
- craft knife (WITH ADULT HELP) or scissors
- fabric paint
- sponge paintbrush
- pillow

**1** Plan your pillowcase **design**. Draw it on paper.

**2** Fit the cardboard into the pillowcase.

**3** Draw your **design** from step 1 on poster board. Cut out each element. These are your **stencils**.

**4** Place one stencil on the pillowcase. Sponge paint inside the stencil with **fabric** paint. Remove the stencil and let the paint dry. Repeat this step with all stencils that will use the same color paint. Allow each letter or design to dry before adding another.

**5** Complete your design with other paint colors and stencils. Let the paint dry.

**6** Remove the cardboard from the pillowcase. Read the fabric paint label. Follow its instructions to wash the pillowcase before use. Your printed work is ready for sweet dreams!

# PHOTOSENSITIVE NATURE PRINTS

Turn nature into art with special paper! Leaves and flowers become funky printed images.

## MATERIALS
- ✓ leaves, stems, flowers, or other bits of nature
- ✓ photosensitive paper
- ✓ rocks (optional)
- ✓ small tub or bin
- ✓ water
- ✓ towel

**1** Collect interesting bits of nature. Look for cool patterns and shapes.

**2** Lay sheets of photosensitive paper outside in the sun. Arrange your nature items on the papers. Is it windy? Place rocks on the bits of nature. This will keep them from blowing away!

**3** Read the instructions on the paper package. Let your art sit for the listed time.

**4** Fill the small tub or bin with water. Remove the nature bits and lay the papers in the water. Let them **soak** for the length of time listed on the paper package.

**5** Remove the papers from the water. Lay them on the towel and let them dry. Your artworks are ready to display! Frame them, hang them in your locker, or make a **mural**.

# HAND-CARVED STAMP ART

## MATERIALS
- ✔ pencil
- ✔ rubber carving block
- ✔ carving tool set
- ✔ acrylic paints
- ✔ paintbrushes
- ✔ canvas & frame set
- ✔ paper plates
- ✔ craft stick
- ✔ brayer
- ✔ water
- ✔ washcloth

Stamping is a simple printing **technique**. Carve your own stamp to print a **design** again and again!

 Use pencil to draw a shape on the rubber carving block. Use the knife or flat carving tool to cut out the shape.

**2** Use the scoop-shaped carving tools to add **texture** to your cutout.

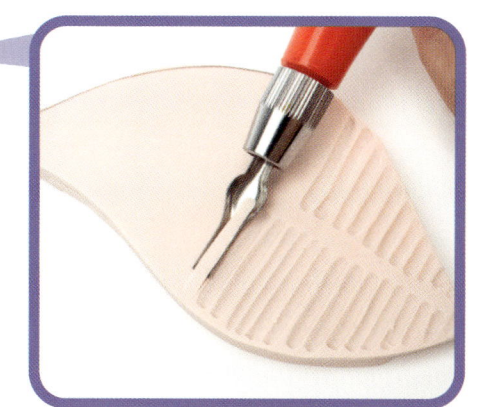

**3** Paint the **canvas**. Let the paint dry. Place the canvas in the frame.

**4** Pour small amounts of two paint colors on a paper plate. Use a craft stick to slightly mix them. Roll the paint out with the brayer.

**5** Use the brayer to coat your stamp in paint. Stamp the canvas and frame. Add more paint to the stamp as needed. Let the paint dry.

**6** Clean and dry the stamp and brayer with water and a washcloth.

**7** Repeat steps 4 through 6 with other colors of paint. When you're happy with your stamp art, put it on display!

# EBRU T-SHIRT

Ebru is a Turkish **marbling technique**. It is often used on **fabric**. Add style to a plain T-shirt with an Ebru-style print!

## MATERIALS
- ✔ water
- ✔ small tub or bin
- ✔ marbling fabric printing kit
- ✔ plain light-colored T-shirt
- ✔ masking tape
- ✔ old towel

**1** Fill the small tub with water.

**2** Squeeze drops of paint across the top of the water.

**3** Find the combing tool in the **marbling** kit. Use it to gently swirl the paints on top of the water.

**4** Fold the shirt so only the part you want to dye faces up. Tape the folds in place.

**5** Flip the shirt so the part to dye faces the water. Slowly lower the shirt to rest on top of the water. Try to make contact with the water evenly and all at once. This will prevent **disturbing** the pattern on the water.

**6** Let the shirt **soak** for the time listed in the marbling kit instructions. Remove the shirt. Lay it faceup on an old towel to dry.

**7** Wash the shirt according to the marbling kit's instructions. Your printed shirt is ready to wear!

## SCIENCE FACT

Most marbling paints are oily. Oil has a lower **density** than water. This allows it to float on the water. Oil is also hydrophobic. This means it **repels** water rather than mixing with it. These features allow marbling paints to sit atop water.

# HOT GLUE STAMPS

## MATERIALS
- paper
- colored pencils
- hot glue gun
- wood blocks
- craft knife (optional) (WITH ADULT HELP)
- ink pad or fabric ink
- paper or fabric
- water

Make your own art supplies! Turn wood and glue into woodblock stamps with fun **designs**.

**1** Plan your stamps! Draw **designs** for each one on paper.

**2** Draw your designs onto the wood blocks using hot glue. If you make a mistake, wait for the glue to dry. Then use a craft knife to carefully peel up the area to fix. Add more glue to finish the design. Let the glue dry.

**3** Look closely at each stamp. Remove any unwanted strings of hot glue.

**4** Dip your stamps in ink. Then press them onto paper or **fabric**!

**5** Rinse your stamps gently and let them dry before using them again. See the next page for a cool idea for using your stamps!

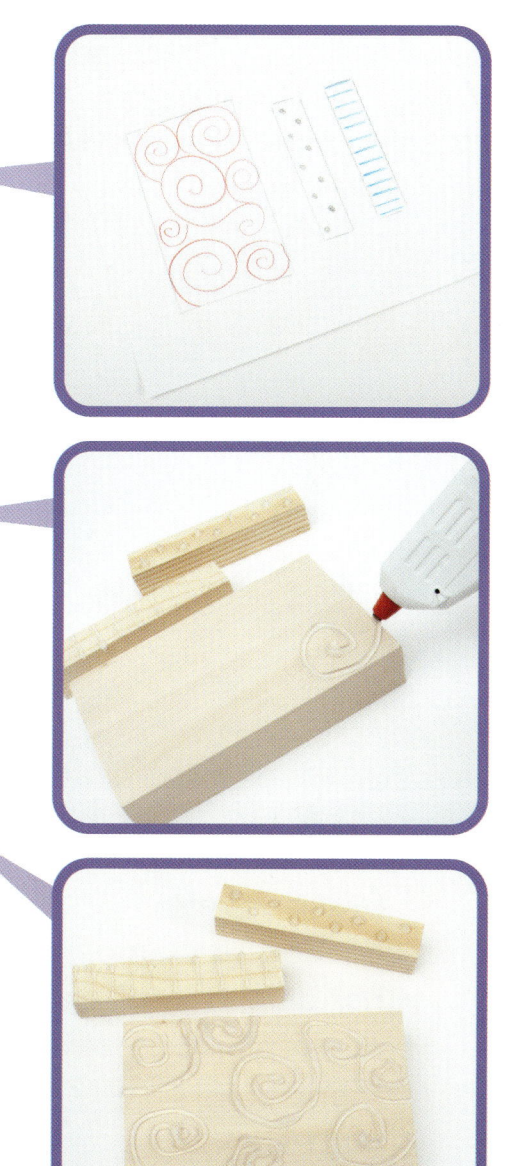

# STAMP BANDANNA

Put your handmade stamps to use! Cover **fabric** with a block pattern to make a bandanna.

## MATERIALS
- fabric square
- decorative stamps, such as the hot glue stamps on page 22
- paper plates
- fabric paints
- craft sticks
- water for rinsing (optional)

**1** Lay the **fabric** square flat on your workspace.

**2** Pour one color of fabric paint onto a paper plate. Spread it out with a craft stick.

**3** Dip a stamp in the paint. Then stamp it onto the fabric. Continue dipping the stamp in paint and stamping the fabric. Create a pattern!

**4** Pour another color of paint onto a plate and spread it out with a craft stick.

**5** Dip another stamp in the new paint color and onto the fabric. Or, rinse the previous stamp and reuse it! Continue dipping the stamp in paint and stamping the fabric to add to your pattern.

**6** Repeat steps 4 and 5 with more colors of paint if you'd like. Let the paint dry. Then, wear your bandanna or hang it up as a work of art!

# SCREEN PRINTING STENCIL

Screen printing involves pushing ink through **stencils** and onto silk screens. Create a screen printing stencil. Use it to add a **design** to all sorts of items!

## MATERIALS
- paper
- pencil
- clear contact paper
- tape
- craft knife (WITH ADULT HELP)
- screen printer's frame
- painter's tape

1. Plan your **stencil** on paper. Draw a simple **design** you would like to screen print.

2. Tape a sheet of clear contact paper to your drawing. Use a craft knife to cut the design out of the contact paper.

3. Separate the paper and contact paper. Remove the contact paper's backing. Stick the contact paper onto the printing screen within the frame.

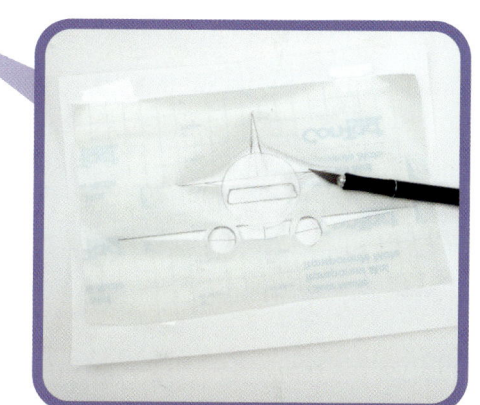

4. Place painter's tape along the frame's edge where it meets the screen. Close any gaps. This will keep ink from being pressed through the edges of the frame.

5. Your stencil is ready to use! Turn to page 28 for directions on using it to make a T-shirt.

# SCREEN-PRINTED T-SHIRT

Show off your DIY skills on a screen-printed T-shirt of your own **design!**

## MATERIALS
- ✔ cardboard
- ✔ plain T-shirt
- ✔ screen printing stencil (see page 26)
- ✔ sponge brush
- ✔ paper plate
- ✔ fabric paint

1. Slide the cardboard into the T-shirt. This will hold the shirt flat. It will also keep paint from **soaking** through to the other side of the shirt.

2. Set your screen printing **stencil** on the shirt where you want your **design** to appear.

3. Pour **fabric** paint onto the paper plate.

4. Sponge paint the stencil to **transfer** the design to the shirt. Let the paint dry.

5. Wash your shirt according to the instructions on the fabric paint label before wearing it.

## SCIENCE FACT

Some screen printers use photo emulsion. This is a light-sensitive liquid. Printers coat the screens with photo emulsion. Then they use black tape to create designs on clear paper. They tape the paper onto the screens and set them in bright light. The light hardens the liquid except where it is covered by the tape. The screen becomes a stencil!

# KEEP CRAFTING

Push your projects past ordinary. Keep crafting to make your creations EXTRAORDINARY!

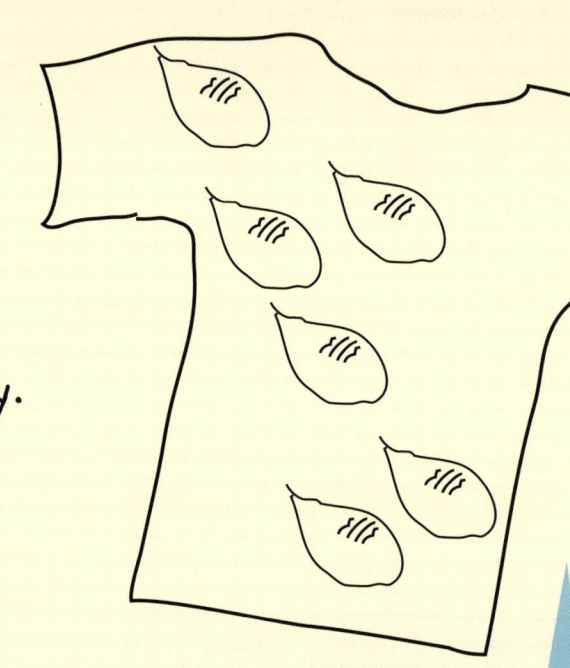

Use your stamp from page 18 on **fabric**! Stamp shirts, tote bags, and more.

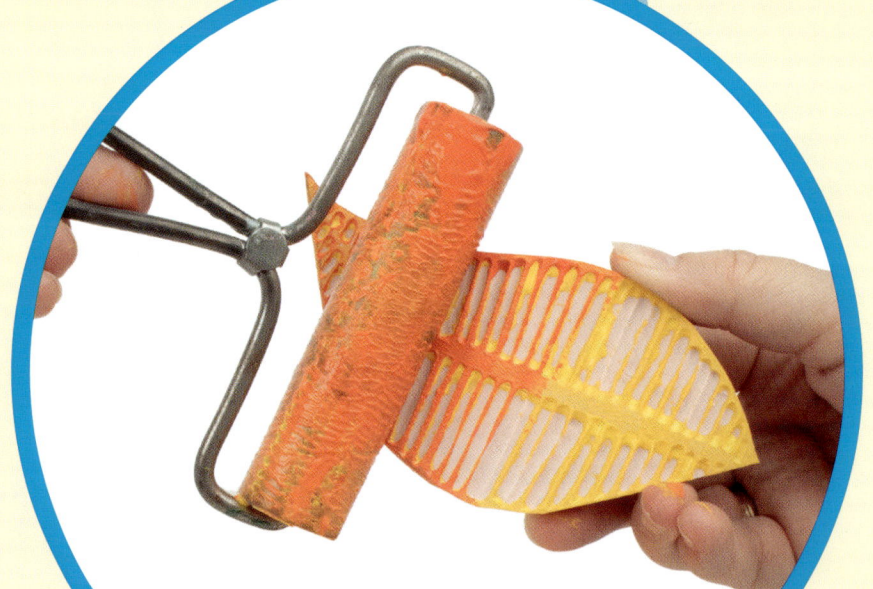

Try the **marbling technique** from page 20 on more items! Marble sheets of craft paper or card stock.

Create more **stencils** to add to your shirt from page 28. Screen print a frame or other **designs**. Or, add designs using a stamp from page 22!

# GLOSSARY

**canvas**–a type of thick cloth that is often on a frame for artists to paint on.

**cylinder**–a solid, round shape with flat ends. A soda can is a cylinder.

**density**–how much mass something has compared to the amount of space it takes up.

**design**–a decorative pattern or arrangement.

**engrave**–to cut or carve figures, letters, or designs into a hard surface.

**etch**–to make a design on a hard surface using either a sharp instrument or a substance that eats into the surface. A combination of both methods may also be used.

**fabric**–woven material or cloth.

**linoleum**–a smooth material made of layers of dried linseed oil.

**marbling**–making something look like marble, a type of stone.

**mural**–a large piece of art that is often displayed on a wall or ceiling.

**repel**–to cause something to move away.

**soak**–to leave something in a liquid for a while.

**stencil**–a flat piece of material with a cutout.

**technique**–a way of doing something.

**texture**–a rough or uneven feel or appearance.

**traditional**–the way something has been done by the people in a particular group, family, or society for a long time.

**transfer**–to pass from one thing or place to another.